AF421810

Fly Away
Written by Tommy Watkins

Today is the day
to launch off this tree and fly
away.

Mother will be sad, but here's my chance to see the world.

I spread my wings, ready to lift off! My wings stop working and I nearly face plant on the ground.

As the sun sets, I am still on the tree. No way is this happening, tomorrow has to be the day to fly.

The next morning, Mother wakes me up saying it's time to fly away

With Mother watching me,
I use all my strength and start
flapping my wings.

I launch off the tree and into the sky!

Mother watched me fly away with
a tear in her eye.

The End